Bibliographic information published by the German National Library:

The German National Library lists this publication in the National Bibliography; detailed bibliographic data are available on the Internet at http://dnb.dnb.de .

Imprint:

Copyright © 2015 GRIN Verlag, Open Publishing GmbH
Print and binding: Books on Demand GmbH, Norderstedt Germany
ISBN: 9783668225084

Mohamed Sghir Syad

A Critique of Monist Afrocentrism in Toni Morrison's "Paradise"

GRIN Publishing

GRIN - Your knowledge has value

Since its foundation in 1998, GRIN has specialized in publishing academic texts by students, college teachers and other academics as e-book and printed book. The website www.grin.com is an ideal platform for presenting term papers, final papers, scientific essays, dissertations and specialist books.

Visit us on the internet:

http://www.grin.com/

http://www.facebook.com/grincom

http://www.twitter.com/grin_com

A Critique of Monist Afrocentrism in Toni Morrison's *Paradise* (1998)

First coined by W.E.B. Du Bois in the early 1960s then popularised by Asante a couple of decades later, the term Afrocentrism represents a talking back against the hegemonic attitudes and discourses that have been disfiguring and marginalising the African Americans' cultural legacies and historical realities both before and after the Transatlantic Passage.[1] As Wilson Jeremiah Moses points out, the rise of Afrocentrism is a reaction to disparaging stereotypes that "doubt the capacity of black people for 'civilization,' meaning self-government, mechanical invention, economic independence, and abstract reasoning."[2] Early American politicians, intellectuals, and slave-owners classified black people as biologically and intellectually of a lower rank than Caucasians. Thomas Jefferson, for example, could write that:

> This unfortunate difference of color and perhaps of faculty is a powerful obstacle to the emancipation of these people.... I advance it therefore as a suspicion only that the blacks whether originally a distinct race or made distinct by time and circumstances, are inferior to the whites in the endowments of the mind and body.[3]

In the face of such cultural racism, Afrocentrists, such as Du Bois, Marcus Garvey, Elijah Mohammad, Malcolm X, Ron Karenga, Ivan Van Sertima, and Molefi Kete Asante, to name but a few, attempted to promote and consolidate African- and African American-based forms of knowledge to convey the urgent need for the rehabilitation of Africans and African Americans. In the words of Asante:

> Afrocentricity seeks to re-locate the African person as an agent in human history in an effort to eliminate the illusion of the fringes. For the past five hundred years Africans have been taken off of cultural, economic, religious, political, and social terms and have existed primarily on the periphery of Europe.[4]

In rewriting her people's history in *Paradise*,[5] Morrison touches upon the issue of Afrocentrism as a cornerstone in the social, political and cultural understanding of black America. Her steadfast interest in black peoples' lives and destinies may be read as a self-evident concern with Afrocentrism. Both her literary art and cultural criticism overlap, in one way or another, with moderate forms of Afrocentrism. As a case in point, "Recitatif" evokes the writer's convergence with an alternative Afrocentric

---

[1] Wilson Jeremiah Moses, *Afrotopia: The Roots of African American Popular History* (Cambridge: Cambridge University Press, 1998), 1-2.
[2] Ibid., 21.
[3] Molefi Kete Asante, *Afrocentricity: The Theory of Social Change* (Buffalo, NY: Amulefi Publishing Co., 1980), 43.
[4] Ibid., 37.
[5] Toni Morrison, *Paradise* (New York: Plume, 1999). Future references are to this edition and will be cited parenthetically.

1

feminist epistemology, as articulated in Patricia Hill Collins' essay "The Social Construction of Black Feminist Thought."[6] Similarly and to the credit of Afrocentrism, one of the main points that her introductory essay in *Race-ing Justice, En-gendering Power* analyses is Eurocentric distorted and distorting knowledge of black people. She critiques how racial stereotypes disseminate essentialist fictions about blacks in America: "On the one hand, they signify benevolence, harmless and servile guardianship, and endless love. On the other hand, they have come to represent insanity, illicit sexuality, and chaos."[7] To Morrison, these stereotypical dichotomies form a superficial, prejudicial oversimplification of real meaning, which is, of course, always dependent on context, relationship, and perspective.

Many of Afrocentrism's beliefs, especially the common origins of African cultures, the distinctive epistemologies of African civilisations, and the cultural contribution of black peoples to today's Western societies relate back to 1960s and 1970s black political and cultural nationalism.[8] Correspondingly, the temporal setting of *Paradise* extends across a critical historical period of 1968 to 1976, which, suggestively, marks, first, the escalation of the Vietnam War in which blacks were disproportionately sent to deadly frontlines and, second, the rise of Black Power that overtook the Civil Rights Movement. In the 1960s when America underwent upheavals at home and military crises abroad, blacks demanded their rights. Met with a violent white extremist backlash, black movements, like Black Muslims and Black Panthers, called for racial separatism.[9] They nourished the idea that their people's positive identity resided in their return to their resources, either morally by identifying with African-based views of the world and systems of thought or physically by actually returning to Africa as a place of hope and promise. In his reading of *Paradise* in terms of history and race, Peter Widdowson refers to the warning that the final report of the National Advisory Committee on Civil Disorders in March 1968 issued:

> Our nation is moving toward two societies, one black, one white—separate and unequal.... What white Americans have never fully understood—but what the Negro can never forget—is that white

---

[6] Patricia Hill Collins, "The Social Construction of Black Feminist Thought," in Malson et al., *Black Women in America*, 297-325. In her narration of the story, Twyla embraces the four dimensions of Afrocentric feminist epistemology as expounded by Collins: 1) concrete experience as praxis for attaining and claiming knowledge and truth, 2) dialogic interaction as a means of communal connectedness, 3) the ethic of caring and fellow-feeling, and 4) the ethic of personal accountability.
[7] Morrison, "Introduction: Friday on the Potomac," xv.
[8] Stephen Howe, *Afrocentrism: Mythical Pasts and Imagined Homes* (London: Verso, 1999), 265.
[9] Widdowson, "The American Dream Refashioned," 326.

2

society is deeply implicated in the ghetto. White institutions created it, white institutions maintain it, and white society condones it.[10]

Losing hope of receiving more than minimal integration in mainstream America, black separatists wanted to undertake their own economic, political social and religious sustenance and self-empowerment. In a similar sense, *Paradise* presents the Ruby people attempting to maintain their difference from other communities. When Morrison describes them as "different from other communities in only a couple of ways: beauty and isolation" (*P* 160), she alludes to the psycho-cultural Afrocentric slogans of Black pride and Black beauty. However, in her approach to Afrocentrism Morrison is aware of the "New Black Psychology"[11] agenda of creating positive black self-images and promoting the demand for the recovery of collective black culture, and the group of 1960s black radical psychologists whose "wild" Afrocentric views pontificated about the existence of "a distinctive 'black personality'" and an "inherent black psychic superiority."[12] In point of fact, her attitude toward the Rubyites' sense of Afrocentrism is marked by irony. She channels that irony by juxtaposing the sense of their beauty with that of their isolation. Here, Morrison seems to signify on *The Bluest Eye*—but in a very differently inflected fashion. In that novel Pauline Breedlove understands beauty in terms of white culture and shuns the ancient properties of her own, identical people, unlike the Rubyites' sense of beauty and isolation. If the cult of beauty, in *Paradise*, is a commendable objective to abolish centuries of ill-founded physiognomic and epidermal judgments, the choice of isolation and exclusionism is criticised for it cuts off all possibilities and chances for dialogue and rapprochement. Thus, the Rubyite patriarchs' sense of racial purity and moral superiority comes down, unfortunately, to their own self-aggrandizement, the attitude that convicts them of reiterating the same ethnocentric purist biases against which they originally fought. Morrison is quite clear in voicing her dissension from such inverse deep blue-black ethnocentric racism when she writes:

> They [the Ruby patriarchs] think they have outfoxed the white men when in fact they imitate him. They think they are protecting their wives and children, when in fact they are maiming them. [...] Born out of an old hatred, one that began when one kind of black man scorned another kind and that kind took the hatred to another level, their selfishness had trashed two hundred years of suffering and triumph in a moment of such pomposity and error and callousness it froze the mind [...] Soon Ruby will be like any other country town: the young thinking of elsewhere; the old full of regret. (*P* 306)

---

[10] Ibid., 327.
[11] Howe, *Afrocentrism*, 265.
[12] Ibid., 265-266.

Through Reverend Misner's judgmental lamentation, she expresses her critique of racial divisions that make people blind and unprepared to face the future. With such divisions the progeny enters a distorted, maimed history fraught with ethnic and racial hatred that absolutely cannot reinforce the human values of mutual respect and tolerance.

Morrison articulates her rejection of strong or "wild" Afrocentrism. She doubts its efficacy because its appeal to intellectual separatism and cultural nationalism is more disabling than enabling and its characteristics are, in the words of Stephen Howe, "barriers to or digressions from the development of effective strategies against racism and for social justice."[13] Asante, alias Arthur Lee Smith, is one of the proponents of strong forms of Afrocentrism. His overenthusiastic Afrocentric "delinking"[14] leads him to conceive Africans as one whole group disregarding in this way ethnic, racial, gender, class, historical, national and cultural differences. He admits "Regardless of our various complexions and degrees of consciousness we are by virtue of commitments, history, and convictions an African people."[15] Addressing blacks the world over, Asante asserts "there can be but one true objective for us in the contemporary era [:] to reconstruct our lives on an Afrocentric base."[16] Asante's short-sightedness in his presentation of Blacks as essentially one homogeneous group of people with one past, or history, deflates his Afrocentric perspective as an idealised understanding that risks turning black peoples' cultures into Black Culture. His idea of a recoverable tradition overlooks the fact that both identity and tradition are cultural constructs that are liable to change in accordance to different historical moments and ideological interests. Asante's essentialist model of Afrocentricity is undercut by Eric Wolf's statement that cultures are not

> [I]ntegrated totalities in which each part contributes to the maintenance of an organized, autonomous, and enduring whole. There are only cultural sets of practices and ideas, put into play by determinate human actors under determinate circumstances. In the course of action, these cultural sets are forever assembled, dismantled, and reassembled, conveying in variable accents the divergent paths of groups and classes.[17]

Asante is blind to the fact that traditions, when they are the constructs of the ruling classes, become an impediment to any form of emancipation or ethnic identity protection. As Michel Foucault observes, any project of total history is inclined to ignore micro-narratives

---

[13] Howe, *Afrocentrism*, 5.

[14] Ibid., 234.

[15] Asante, *Afrocentricity*, 27.

[16] Ibid., 85.

[17] Eric Wolf, *Europe and the People Without History* (Berkeley: University of California P, 1982), 390-91.

and thus puts a curb on voices that would disrupt the apparent continuum of macro-narratives set and claimed by the project of historical totality.[18] In the novel the patriarchs of Ruby preclude themselves from any chance to move away from the inherited traditions of their ancestors. They keep to their Old Fathers' passed-on memories and commandments as if they were sacred inscriptions never to be questioned.

It is quite significant that Morrison does not use Patricia to level her criticism of the community's blind attachment to past traditions. Though Patricia is conscious of her undesirability in the deep blue-black community, she does not seem to question a sense of tradition. She decries the patriarchs' unyielding exclusionism, but does not urge for change from their inherited traditions: "She didn't seem to trust these Ruby hardheads with the future […], but neither did she encourage change" (*P* 209). It is Reverend Misner, a newcomer and outsider, who is made to express Morrison's critique of such people:

> Over and over and with the least provocation, they [the Ruby patriarchs] pulled from their stock of stories tales about the old folks, their grands and great-grands; their fathers and mothers. […] why were there no stories to tell of themselves? And about their own lives they shut up. Had nothing to say, pass on. As though past heroism was enough of a future to live by. As though, rather than children, they wanted duplicates. (*P* 161)

To the Reverend, the Ruby patriarchs seem to live and rely on the deeds and traditions of their past forefathers. The present, for them, is overlooked since the past is directly linked to their future. This defective historical dependence on the Old Fathers' traditions is accountable for the present disruption of the community. Symbolic of this crisis is, indeed, the course of Steward's life which is, as his wife Dovey acknowledges, replete with a series of losses: from personal gustatory blandness to a religious loss of calling, from political ineptitude to business decline, and from biological sterility to physiognomic unattractiveness (*P* 82).

Although Reverend Misner and Patricia Best are presented as sharing much in their critique of the Rubyites, Morrison depicts them as holding different attitudes toward Afrocentrism. Patricia expresses her desire to implant and assert her own self on the American soil while Misner argues for a return to the sources—some pre-Middle Passage Africa—as the most valid way to assert his African-related identity, values and immaculate past: "There was a whole lot of life before slavery. And we ought to know

---

[18] Michel Foucault, *The Archaeology of Knowledge and the Discourse on Language*, trans. A.M. Sheridan Smith (New York: Pantheon, 1972), 9.

what it is. If we're going to get rid of the slave mentality, that is" (*P* 210). In his efforts to advance and perform an emancipatory project, Reverend Misner finally succumbs to cultural nationalism and idealism, not dissimilar to Asante's and other fervent Afrocentrists'. Misner suggests to Patricia that those black Americans who think they have nothing to do with Africa are "never going to get rid of the slave mentality" (*P* 210).

In response to his essentialist attitude, which concurs with Afrocentric nationalists who seek to recover their authentic past, free of its scars, Patricia sees that "the slave mentality" Misner tries to avoid as essential to understanding the blacks of America. The attempt to ignore it is a mis-recognition of the matter. For Patricia, the hankering of African Americans for a slave-free past is absurd: present-day Africans do not see themselves as having anything in common with blacks of America. Having an African name, wearing African clothes, choosing an African hairstyle, or embracing an African religion has nothing to do with the erasure of four centuries of slavery. Patricia's view sounds similar to Pamela A. Keels, an African American who worked for health-care in Uganda and who witnessed the difference between black Americans' held beliefs about Africa and the reality in Africa. Understanding that Afrocentricity does not help African Americans to enhance their awareness of continental African reality, she states that:

> We must explain to our children that locks are not a Pan-African tradition, that not all Africans understand or desire to bond with African Americans and that we have created many of the concepts of Afrocentricity from a patchwork of various African histories and cultures. More important, I realized that we must examine all our information sources and knowledge of Africa to determine how Afrocentricity relates to our current situation–both in America and on the African continent.[19]

Therefore, in this experiential analysis it is rather the self-conscious will to implement a revolutionary change at the level of the individual self first then the communal self. Admittedly, when she forms a riposte to Misner's argument for a return to origins, Patricia grasps that such desire for a slave-free past is a mere smokescreen to avoid the reality of slavery. Instead, she courageously affirms that "slavery is our past, nothing can change that," adding, "certainly not Africa" (*P* 210). Slavery, despicable as it is, is a crucial chapter in her people's history. To miss or overlook it is to condemn them to perpetual repetition of its effects and different present new forms. For Patricia, then, slavery becomes the first stage to freedom.

---

[19] Pamela A. Keels, "Afrocentricity: The Real Deal," *Essence Magazine* 26, no. 3 (July 1995): 116.

Blinded by the Afrocentric idealism that reproduces all the features of "ethnonationalism,"[20] Asante exposes himself to contradictions.[21] He views Afrocentric identity as closely bound up with black skin as well as with colour-blindness. That is, while he speaks of Afrocentricity as being "not a matter of color but of culture,"[22] he defines the Afrocentric reality in terms of epidermal blackness.[23] Similarly, in the novel, Misner embodies a contradictory position: although he seems not to share the Ruby patriarchs' exclusionism on the grounds of race and specifically colour, he also aspires to an exclusive identification with people in Africa as the latter is the place of origin. For him, skin is closely related to geography and history, the view that Patricia deflates thoughtfully when she refers to race-suffering people all over the world:

> You want some foreign Negroes to identify with, why not South America? Or Germany, for that matter. They have brown babies over there you could have a good time connecting with. Or is it just some kind of past with no slavery in it you're looking for? (*P* 210)

Patricia, in contradistinction with Misner's ethnonationalist tendency, sees identification with Africa, as Afrocentricity, as ineffective because it is limited and limiting. Instead, she suggests her concern for Black diasporas all over the world, and idea that echoes Stuart Hall's critique of "strong Afrocentrism":

> Africa is not waiting there in the fifteenth or seventeenth century, waiting for you to roll back across the Atlantic and rediscover it in its tribal purity, waiting there in its prelogical mentality, waiting to be woken from inside by its returning sons and daughters.[24]

Though Morrison does not trust "either/or" solutions[25] concerning Afrocentric notions of racial isolationism or racial or national integration, her characters are depicted as representing the oppositional stance of Booker T. Washington and W.E.B. Du Bois. The leading elders of Ruby appear to follow Washington's recommendation of boosting their racial pride and developing their sense of economic self-reliance as a philosophy of progress, which accommodates industrial education, racial solidarity, self-help and, above all, emphatically, racial segregation. It receives its full application in Ruby and before it in Haven. Showing their industriousness and volition to support themselves by themselves, Morrison's narrator states, "they, of all people, knew the necessity of unalloyed will; the rewards of courage and single-mindedness. Of all people, they

---

[20] Howe, *Afrocentrism*, 1.
[21] Ibid., 16.
[22] Asante, *Afrocentricity*, 41.
[23] Ibid., 42.
[24] Stuart Hall, "Negotiating Caribbean Identities," *New Left Review* 209, no. 1 (January-February 1995): 11. 3-14, quoted in Howe, *Afrocentrism*, 13.
[25] Carol Shields, "Heaven On Earth" *The Washington Post*, 11 January 1998, X01.

understood the mechanisms of wresting power" (*P* 161). Indisputably, will, courage, focus and power are the four qualities behind the survival of the all-black town. However, as Reverend Misner observes, such qualities produce a boomerang, adverse effect in the youth's desire for change. The elders do not admit to the fact that their youth join the national resistance movements against racism; for they seem to have experienced internal racism and at the same time to have got keep themselves isolated from both whites and the light-skinned.

The elders of Ruby are totally indifferent to Du Bois' idea of "double consciousness." They live in accordance to their moral and racial purity. Instead of double consciousness, they live in accordance with a race consciousness. They know they are deep blue-black and they know they have been rejected on that ground. They do not see themselves as struggling to identify themselves as integrative American subjects, for they have been disillusioned by the repeated social and political disappointments. They belong to a set of black patriarchs who have been in America for more than two centuries:

> Descendants of those who had been in Louisiana Territory when it was French, when it was Spanish, when it was French again, when it was sold to Jefferson and when it became a state in 1812. Who spoke a patois part Spanish, part French, part English, and all their own. Descendants of those who, after the Civil war, had defied or hidden from whites doing all they could to force them to stay and work as sharecroppers in Louisiana. Descendants of those whose worthiness was so endemic it got three of their children elected to rule in state legislatures and county offices: who, when thrown out of office without ceremony or proof of wrongdoing, refused to believe what they guessed was the real reason that made it impossible for them to find other mental labor. Almost all of the Negro men chased or invited out of office [in Mississippi, in Louisiana, in Georgia] got less influential but still white-collar work following the purges of 1875. One from South Carolina ended his days as a street sweeper. But they alone [Zechariah Morgan and Juvenal DuPres in Louisiana, Drum Blackhorse in Mississippi] were reduced to penury and/or field labor. Fifteen years of begging for sweat work in cotton, lumber or rice after five glorious years remaking a country. They must have suspected yet dared not say that their misfortune's misfortune was due to the one and only feature that distinguished them from their Negro peers. (*P* 193)

In this sense Morrison historicizes them most carefully. Their ancestors witness and contribute to the founding and development of the US long before many other settlers and immigrants. Their people are never under the direct power of the British government. The passage also alludes to the failure of Reconstruction. Despite the emancipation from slavery after 1865, Southern whites fortified and consolidated their racial superiority, a situation against which federal law failed to impose itself.

Unlike their patriarchs, the young generation in Ruby appears to embrace Du Bois' demand for socio-economic equality to whites. The young people look forward to mixing with the rest of the world on an equal basis. For such purposes, as the novel suggests, the young join national resistance movements against racism. The raised fist graffiti on the Oven indicate the influence of black power consciousness on the youth that their fathers condemn as a sign of the collapse of ancient values, morals and stability. For the Morgans, as for the old generation, the painting on the oven is a sort of blasphemy against the past. But what is more important is Anna Flood's rubbing of the fist off the oven. Her act does not subscribe to the elders' defence of the past but rather explains her disagreement with violence of all kinds. And Misner, an ex-convict and political pacifist, is presented as sympathising with the young generation.

The recasting of (African) American history in *Paradise*, represented through the multiple contending characters' (hi)stories, voices, and views, demonstrates Morrison's strategic deployment of historical representation from the double perspective of essentialism and anti-essentialism. While she makes use of historical documents as sources for the reconstruction of African American history in her novel, she interrogates totalising conceptions of historical referentiality. That said, Morrison's keen interest in the past and in history sees the possibilities of reclaiming the neglected past of black people in general and black women in particular. She rewrites African American history to restore "the four-hundred-year-old [...] overwhelming presence of black people in the United States"[26] back to the centre of American literature and history.

The multiple stories or histories are made possible by the formal method of open-endedness and polyvocality. When reading what she has written and published, Morrison always confesses her desire to have it otherwise.[27] She is never satisfied with her characters for she knows she can never be final in whatever she has done with them. In respect to the character of Patricia, she has expressed her wish to have another attempt at her. This inclination to "rewrite" Patricia indicates that this character more than any other is the novel's centre of consciousness in regard to the novel's key issues, notably the role of historiography. Much of the history of the townspeople is filtered through her consciousness to the extent that she is regarded as the mouthpiece of the

---

[26] Morrison, *Playing in the Dark*, 5.
[27] Jaffrey, "Toni Morrison," 146.

author's conception of historical recuperation and its representation. However, though it has been said that the throwing of the history project into the flames reflects Patricia's awareness of the difficulty of historical recoverability, it seems for Patricia, as it does for Morrison, that it is always worth attempting to look for the unrecoverable and the unknown, to seize some parts, little as they may be but nevertheless important, to conciliate one's past, one's people and, above all, one's self.

Bibliography

Asante, Molefi Kete. *Afrocentricity: The Theory of Social Change*. Buffalo, NY: Amulefi Publishing Co., 1980.

Collins, Patricia Hill. "The Social Construction of Black Feminist Thought." In *Black Women in America: Social Science Perspectives*. Edited by Michelin R. Malson et al., 297-325. Chicago: University of Chicago Press, 1990.

Foucault, Michel. *The Archaeology of Knowledge and the Discourse on Language*. Translated by. A.M. Sheridan Smith. New York: Pantheon, 1972.

Hall, Stuart. "Negotiating Caribbean Identities." *New Left Review* 209, no. 1 (January-February 1995): 3-14. Quoted in Stephen Howe, *Afrocentrism: Mythical Pasts and Imagined Homes*. London: Verso, 1999.

Howe, Stephen. *Afrocentrism: Mythical Pasts and Imagined Homes*. London: Verso, 1999.

Jaffrey, Zia. "Toni Morrison/1998." In *Toni Morrison: Conversations*. Edited Carolyn C. Denard, 139-154. Jackson: Mississippi University Press, 2008.

Keels, Pamela A. "Afrocentricity: The Real Deal," *Essence Magazine* 26, no. 3 (July 1995): 116-117.

Morrison, Toni. "Introduction: Friday on the Potomac." In *Race-ing Justice, En-gendering Power: Essays on Anita Hill, Thomas Clarence, and the Construction of Social Reality*. Edited by Toni Morrison, vii-xxx. New York: Pantheon Books, 1992.

------. *Paradise*. New York: Plume, 1999.

------. *Playing in the Dark: Whiteness and the Literary Imagination*. London and Basingstoke: Picador, 1993.

Moses, Wilson Jeremiah. *Afrotopia: The Roots of African American Popular History*. Cambridge: Cambridge University Press, 1998.

Shields, Carol. "Heaven On Earth." *The Washington Post*. 11 January 1998, X01.

Widdowson, Peter. "The American Dream Refashioned: History, Politics and Gender in Toni Morrison's *Paradise*." *Journal of American Studies* 35, no. 2 (2001): 313-335.

Wolf, Eric. *Europe and the People Without History*. Berkeley: University of California Press, 1982.

YOUR KNOWLEDGE HAS VALUE